ISABELLE EBERHARDT

THE OBLIVION SEEKERS

Translated from the French and with a preface
by Paul Bowles

PETER OWEN
London and Chester Springs, PA, USA

PETER OWEN PUBLISHERS
73 Kenway Road, London SW5 0RE

Peter Owen books are distributed in the USA by Dufour Editions Inc.,
Chester Springs, PA 19425–0007

The selections in this volume were originally published in French
in *Pages d'Islam* and *Dans l'Ombre Chaude d'Islam*,
Editions Fasquelle, Paris.

The translations of 'Criminal' and 'The Oblivion Seekers' were first
published in *Antaeus*.

First published in Great Britain 1988
Translation and Preface © Paul Bowles 1972, 1975
This paperback edition 2010

ISBN 978-0-7206-1338-4

A catalogue record for this book is available from
the British Library

Printed by CPI Bookmarque Ltd, Croydon, CR0 4TD

For Carol Ardman

CONTENTS

Preface

Isabelle Eberhardt—b. Geneva, Switzerland 1877
d. Ain Sefra, Algeria 1904

Not long before her death Isabelle Eberhardt wrote: "No one ever lived more from day to day than I, or was more dependent upon chance. It is the inescapable chain of events that has brought me to this point, rather than I who have caused these things to happen." Her life seems haphazard, at the mercy of caprice, but her writings prove otherwise. She did not make decisions; she was impelled to take action. Her nature combined an extraordinary singleness of purpose and an equally powerful nostalgia for the unattainable. Over the years the goal imperceptibly changed from the idea of simple escape to the obsession of total freedom, only later manifesting itself in a quest for spiritual wisdom through the discipline of Sufism. Escape and freedom are often the subject matter of her writing; as to Sufism, even if the doctrine had not been a secret one, she had too much humility to consider herself anything more than a neophyte, and so she kept silent about it. Her wisdom lay in knowing that what she sought was unreachable. "We are, all of us, poor wretches, and those who prefer not to understand this are even worse off than the rest of us."

If Alexander Trophimowsky had not taken complete charge of his illegitimate daughter's education and upbringing, no one would ever have heard of Isabelle Eberhardt. By obliging her to perform hard physical labor outdoors alongside her brothers during her childhood and adolescence, he made it possible for her to withstand the rigors of the spartan life she was to live later on. By insisting that she appear regularly, dressed in men's clothing, not only at home but also in public, he assured her the subsequent ease she felt in wearing male disguise, a device which was to prove a *sine qua non* in the Sahara. Had he not bought her a horse and taught her to ride it properly while she was still a child, she would have had no mobility in the desert. He saw to it that she grew up a polyglot, even teaching her to read and write Classical Arabic when she asked for it. Trophimowsky had been a friend of Bakunin and was himself a Nihilist, full of untried theories about education; he allowed his daughter to have no contact with the Swiss among whom they lived. Very early he instilled in her a healthy contempt for the values of bourgeois society. Indifference to public opinion was essential if she was to be able to lead the kind of life she demanded.

It goes without saying that Isabelle did not see these early years in such a comforting light; she dreamed only of escape. First she persuaded her mother to accompany her to Algeria, where they were both officially converted to Islam. Shortly afterward, her mother fell ill. Trophimowsky arrived in North Africa too late to see her alive. He found Isabelle in a state of hysteria, wailing that she too wanted to die. The old Nihilist's reaction was typical: he took out his revolver and offered it to her. She did not accept it.

For a while she lived in Tunis, where her life style aroused the hostility of the French. Certainly her behavior was not one to reassure the prim provincial colonists. At night she could be found lying on the floor of some native café smoking kif or wrestling with the soldiers from the barracks. Often she took one of them home with her to spend the night. She wrote of "a strange desire to suffer, to drag my physical self into dirt and deprivation."

When she returned to Switzerland, hoping to get hold of her mother's property, Trophimowsky himself succumbed to cancer, leaving the house and land to Isabelle. However, he had a wife back in Odessa, and she immediately contested the will. Isabelle never received her legacies. She returned to Tunis, drunk with the prospect of liberty and with very little money, and at once set out for the desert, without any idea of how she would get there or what she would do when she did.[1] Several months later she was back in Tunis in an even worse financial state, and crossed to Marseille to visit her brother, whom she found in a condition of poverty almost as desperate as her own. She continued to Geneva, still with the forlorn hope of being able to arrange her affairs. The property had been seized and the house boarded up, pending a legal settlement. As a last resort she went on to Paris, imagining that she might

[1] See *Diary Notes* for an account of this journey.

somehow manage to make a living as a journalist. (From the beginning she had determined to be a writer.)

Here a great stroke of luck befell her: she met the Marquise de Morès, whose husband had been mysteriously murdered on an expedition in southern Tunisia four years earlier. Madame de Morès wanted details on the death of her husband, and Isabelle seemed to her the ideal person to conduct a secret inquiry. It was agreed between them that the marquise would finance Isabelle's return to North Africa and send her regular sums, and that Isabelle would do her utmost to unearth new facts relating to the murder. It is hard to imagine what would have become of her without this extraordinary stroke of good fortune, but Isabelle does not seem to have marvelled at it. As a Moslem she accepted bad luck and good with equal unconcern. Nothing could happen but that which had been written at the beginning of time.

She agreed to the aristocratic widow's proposal and started southward, not stopping until she got to El Oued. There she rented a house and settled down to write, apparently having forgotten about the mission on which she had been sent. The local French military officers, however, who had been only too content to allow the murder to become a thing of the past since it had occurred in territory under their jurisdiction, learned that the eccentric young foreigner had arrived from Paris in the pay of Madame de Morès, and eyed her with increased distrust. Isabelle took no notice of them. She bought a horse, and set out to explore the desert roundabout, and to build solid friendships with certain

Moslems who lived in the area. She also met Sliman, a young Algerian soldier, with whom she began a profoundly romantic love affair.

Madame de Morès, having learned of what she considered to be Isabelle's betrayal of trust, cut off all funds. At this point Isabelle showed herself to be a true daughter of Trophimowsky. She calmly set out to be initiated into the secret religious cult of the Qadriya, a Sufi brotherhood that wielded enormous political power among the as yet unconquered desert tribes. Under the name of Si Mahmoud Essadi, which she had long ago adopted to go with her male disguise, she was accepted into the Quadriya. They were under no misapprehension as to her sex; but if she chose to dress as a man it was her affair. From then on, no matter where she went, every member of the cult was bound by oath to feed her, give her shelter, or risk his life to protect her. She belonged to the Qadriya.

The difficulty was that there were others besides the Qadriya. The French were more than ever convinced that they had an unusually clever spy in their midst, and were only waiting for a valid pretext to seize her. Other cults, commanding the allegiance of rival tribes, disapproved of her activities on principle. Thus it was that one day as she sat in a courtyard talking with her friends, an unknown man rushed in, drew his sword, and dealt her a terrific blow, with the intention of cleaving her skull in two. Another stroke of luck for Isabelle: the tip of the sword hit a wire clothesline first, so that instead of her head it was her left arm that was split open and nearly severed. When the assailant was captured, he was identified as a Tidjani, and thus automatically as an enemy of the Qadriya. (The cynical French claimed that the man had actually been sent by the local *moqaddem* of the Qadriya, who they said was Isabelle's lover, and who, having tired of her, saw an opportunity for ridding himself of her and at the same time for arranging that the responsibility for her death should fall on the Tidjaniya.)

When she came out of the hospital six weeks later, she left the desert and journeyed up to Batna, where Sliman had been transferred. The French, however, their hearts set on getting her out of Algeria, chose this moment to issue an order expelling her from the country. Since Sliman, as a sergeant in the Spahis, had French citizenship, he applied for permission to marry her, but this was quickly refused. There was nothing for her to do but return to Marseille where her brother still lived, although in even worse poverty than before. She had scarcely arrived there when the French authorities demanded that she return to Algeria as a witness in the trial of the man who had attacked her. They gave her a fourth-class passage back to Constantine, and she set out.

The prosecution asked for the death penalty for the Algerian, but this was reduced in the sentence to life imprisonment. Isabelle protested against the severity of his punishment, but to no avail. During the trial she was handed a mandate which excluded her for all time from entering any part of French North Africa. Once again she was obliged to go back to Marseille. In the port she was fortunate enough to find work as a stevedor. The pay was so low that she was forced to borrow here and there from the Moslem port-workers. What with the damaged muscles of her left arm, she found the heavy work almost more than even she could bear. During the evenings she wrote feverishly on a novel whose subject matter was drawn from her experiences at the port, and wrote innumerable letters to Sliman, urging him to apply for a transfer to Marseille. Eventually the incredible happened, and he arrived.

They were married first at the Hôtel de Ville and then at the Marseille mosque. Isabelle was now legally a French subject, and could no longer be kept out of the colonies. Early in 1902, both of them penniless, they sailed for Algeria, where they lived for a time with Sliman's parents. It was during this time that Isabelle came in contact with Victor Barrucand, the Anarchist editor of *Les Nouvelles*, one of Algiers' dailies. At the time of her trial this newspaper had been the only one to carry anything but attacks against her. Barrucand recognized her ability, and commissioned a series of articles from her. Moreover, he used his influence to see that Sliman was given a better-paying job as secretary-interpreter at Ténès. Here for a few months her life was a happy one. But the French colonists, enraged that through a mere technicality she had once again gained access to what they considered their fatherland, continued full-force with their campaign of poison-pen letters against her to both the government and the press, with the result that in the end there was a huge scandal in which the Mayor of Ténès, who had befriended her, was forced to resign, and Sliman was removed to a post in an obscure village, while Isabelle, as usual suffering with the various fevers she had contracted, went to stay in Algiers.

Once again Barrucand provided a way out. In the wake of a series of important military engagements between the French and the tribes of Southern Algeria, the press was sending correspondents to report troop movements there. Barrucand was about to inaugurate a new paper called *Akhbar*, for which he proposed that Isabelle serve as war correspondent. Overjoyed, she made the journey to Ain Sefra. This was the headquarters where Lyautey (at that time only a colonel) was planning a vast new campaign that would bring all that part of the Sahara, as well as eastern Morocco, under French domination.

In Ain Sefra Isabelle spent her evenings at the canteen of the Foreign Legion and slept on the floor in the Arab cafés of the town. She and Lyautey became firm friends. Later he wrote of her: "She was what attracts me more than anything else: a rebel. What a delight to find someone who is truly himself, who rejects prejudice, servitude, banality, and who moves through life as freely as a bird through the air." At the same time he saw the use to which he could put her special talents and knowledge. Perhaps to counteract the rumor that she had become his mistress, for long periods of time he would refuse to see her when she called to beg for a little money to buy oats for her horse. Nevertheless they remained on the best of terms, for in Ain Sefra she was at his mercy, and he had a particular plan in mind for which she would be indispensable.

In November 1903 Lyautey wrote General Galliéni a letter which showed that he already had a precise idea of how he would use Isabelle. "It seems to me that the aid of the marabout of Kenadsa . . . would be one of the most important factors in our success." The man to whom he referred, Sidi Brahim ould Mohammed, was the head of the *zaouia*, or monastery, of Kenadsa, a famous center for the propagation of Sufi doctrine, where students congregated from all over North Africa. His prestige and political influence were thus consider-able, and the French could not hope to continue their subjugation of the region without his approval. If he could be persuaded that French occupation was prefer-able to the internecine warfare among the Moslems which kept the entire area in a state of uncertainty and disorder, the French would already have taken a major step toward the attainment of their objective. The diffi-culty was that anti-Christian fanaticism was so intense that no European could get near to Kenadsa.

This, according to Lyautey's scheme, was where Isabelle fitted in. Only she was qualified to enter the town and gain access to the marabout. And since the region of Kenadsa was where she most longed to go, she accepted with enthusiasm. If the ethical discrepancies between Lyautey's ideology and hers were apparent to Isabelle, she showed no sign of giving the matter any thought. It could scarcely have been expected that as a devout Moslem she would agree to become an agent in the cause of Christian imperialism in its struggle to destroy Moslem hegemony. Perhaps in the grip of her obsessive need always to push a little further in the direction of the unknown, she felt that it was she who was using Lyautey rather than the other way around. At all events, she got to Kenadsa, was met by slaves outside the *zaouia*, and promptly found herself locked inside it. After a week of forced inactivity in her cell, she begged for an interview with the marabout. Si Brahim, when he realized that she had not been aware of the strict discipline imposed in Sufi monasteries, agreed to allow her freedom of movement in the region. This was a short-lived consolation, for she soon had a violent and prolonged attack of malaria, which, combined with all the other ailments she had contracted during her wanderings, brought her close to death. Still, even during the long weeks she spent lying on the floor of her cell, whenever she emerged from the periods of delirium, she worked on the manuscript she had begun. When it finally became clear to her that staying any longer at Kenadsa would in all probability cost her her life, she reluctantly left for Ain Sefra. There is no record that she ever broached the subject she had been sent to discuss with the marabout.

On her arrival at Ain Sefra she was taken directly into the military hospital. When she had recovered somewhat, she wrote to Sliman who asked for a leave of absence and made the trip to Ain Sefra. It was agreed that he should rent a small mud house beside the dry river bed where he would live until she was able to leave the hospital and join him.

A day came when she could no longer bear the enforced inactivity of hospital life, and she announced that she was leaving. The doctor tried to make her stay a while longer, but she insisted. Sliman had kif ready for her, and together the two spent a happy night. The next morning, although the weather was clear and sunny, a flash flood came roaring down the river bed with a noise like thunder, destroying the entire lower quarter of the town. Sliman claimed he had seen Isabelle's body being carried downstream along with the scores of other corpses, and Lyautey had his men search far and wide. It was only many days later that they found her, crushed under a beam in the rubble of the house itself, and surrounded by the muddy pages of the manuscript she had been preparing in Kenadsa.

This was in 1904; it was not until 1920 that the book appeared in print, under the title *Dans l'Ombre Chaude de l'Islam*. Much of the manuscript had been swept away by the flood, and much of what remained was illegible. Barrucand pieced the bits together, adding excerpts from letters she had sent him, and even from conversations he remembered having with her. Then he showed the poor taste of appending his name to hers as co-author. In spite of its ambiguous authenticity, it is still a valuable work. (Cecily Mackworth calls it "one of the strangest human documents that a woman has given to the world.") Only two of the pieces in the present collection were taken from that volume: *The Oblivion Seekers* and *The Breath of Night*; the rest are from *Pages d'Islam*.

—*Paul Bowles*

Outside

Long and white, the road twists like a snake toward the far-off blue places, toward the bright edges of the earth. It burns in the sunlight, a dusty stripe between the wheat's dull gold on one side, and the shimmering red hills and grey-green scrub on the other. In the distance, prosperous farms, ruined mud walls, a few huts. Everything seems asleep, stricken by the heat of day. A chanting comes up from the plain, a sound long as the unsheltered road, or as poverty without the hope of change tomorrow, or as weeping that goes unheard. The Kabyl farmers are singing as they work. The pale wheat, the brown barley, lie piled on the earth's flanks, and the earth herself lies back, exhausted by her labor pains.

But all the warm gold spread out in the sunlight causes no glimmer of interest in the uncertain eyes of the wayfarer. His locks are grey, as if covered by the same dull dust that cushions the impact of his bare feet on the earth. He is tall and emaciated, with a sharp profile that juts out from beneath his ragged turban. His grey beard is untended, his eyes cloudy, his lips cracked open by thirst. When he comes to a farm or a hut, he stops and pounds the earth with his long staff of wild olive wood. His raucous voice breaks the silence of the countryside as he asks for Allah's bread. And he is right, the sad-faced wanderer. The sacred bread he demands, without begging for it, is his by right, and the giving of it is only a feeble compensation, a recognizing of the injustice that is in the world.

The wayfarer has no home or family. He goes where he pleases, and his somber gaze encompasses all the vast African landscape. And he leaves the milestones behind, one after the other, as he goes. When the heat is too great and he has had enough walking, he lies down under the big pistachio tree on the side hill, or at the foot of a weeping eucalyptus beside the road. There in the shade he drops into a dreamless sleep.

It may be that at one time it was painful for him to be homeless, to possess nothing, and doubtless also to have to ask for that which his instinct told him was due him in any case. But now, after so many years, each like the last, he has no more desires. He merely undergoes life, indifferent to it.

Often the gendarmes have arrested him and thrown him into prison. But he has never been able to understand, nor has anyone explained to him, how a man can be prohibited from walking in the life-giving light of day, or why those very men who had failed to give him bread or shelter should then tell him that it was *forbidden* not to possess these things.

When they accused him of being a vagabond, always he said the same thing: I haven't stolen. I've done nothing wrong. But they claimed that was not enough, and they would not listen to him. This struck him as unjust, like the signposts along the highways that illiterates had to understand.

The tall, straight back grew bent, and his gait became uncertain. Old age arrived early to exact its payments for his shattered health. He suffered from the wretched illnesses of old age, those ailments whose very cure brings no consolation to the patient, and one day he fell beside the road. Some pious Moslems found him there and carried him to a hospital. He said nothing.

But there the old man of the wide horizons could not bear the white walls, the lack of space. And that spongy bed did not feel as good as the ground that he was used to. He grew depressed and longed for the open road. If he stayed there, he felt, he would merely die, without even the solace of familiar sights around him.

They handed him back his ragged clothes with disgust. He was not able to go very far, and he collapsed before he got out of the city. A policeman came up to him and offered to help him. The old man cried: "If you're a Moslem, leave me alone. I want to die outside. Outside! Leave me alone."

The policeman, with the respect of those of his religion for the penniless and the deranged, went away. The wayfarer dragged himself beyond the hostile city and fell asleep on the soft ground beside a faintly trickling stream. Covered by the friendly dark, and with the vast emptiness around him, he fell into an untroubled sleep. Later, he felt stronger, and he began to walk straight ahead, across the fields and through the scrub.

The night was drawing to an end. A pale glow came up behind the black line of the mountains in Kabylia, and from the farms the cocks' cracked voices called for daylight. He had slept on an embankment which the first rains of autumn had covered with grass. The cyclamen-scented breeze brought with it a penetrating chill. He was weak; a great weariness weighted his arms and legs, but the cough that had come with the arrival of the cold air now bothered him less.

It was daylight. From behind the mountains shone a red dawn, making bloody streaks on the calm surface of the sea, and dyeing the water with golden splotches. The faint mist that still hung above the ravines of Mustapha disappeared, and the countryside came nearer, huge, soft, serene. No broken lines, no clash of color. One would have said that the earth, lying back in exhaustion, still permitted itself a sad and slightly sensual smile. And the wayfarer's arms and legs grew heavier.

He thought of nothing. No desires, no regrets. Softly, in the solitude of the open spaces, the uncomplicated and yet mysterious force that had animated him for so many years, fell asleep inside him. No prayers, no medicines, merely the ineffable happiness of dying.

The first tepid rays of sunlight, filtering through damp veils of eucalyptus leaves, gilded the motionless profile, the closed eyes, the hanging rags, the dusty bare feet and the long olivewood staff: everything that the wayfarer had been. The soul no one suspected him of possessing had been exhaled, a murmur of resignation from ancient Islam, in simple harmony with the melancholy of life.

Blue Jacket

The sound of a bugle playing taps came over the warm night air. The final notes were prolonged almost into a wail; then they died. Quiet stole over the sharp-shooters' barracks. Tired bodies sprawled in confusion, overcome by sleep.

Kaddour Chenoui was not sleeping. He lay on his back, his hot head resting against his bare arms, his untutored mind spinning vague fantasies. He was to be demobilized the following day. So many times during the past four years he had wished for this blessed day. And now that his last night at the barracks had actually arrived, he could not tell whether it was joy or anguish that was making his heart beat with such force.

At fifteen Kaddour had left his father's farm in the Dahra where he had been born, by day to hunt in the wilderness, carrying his uncle's old rifle, and at night in the search for beauties with tattoo marks on their foreheads. He was proud of the scars that cut across his powerful chest and biceps—scars made by knives and stones, and even by firearms—the results of disputes over women who no longer meant anything to him.

Kaddour's father, a poor farmer who believed in inflexible discipline, had not succeeded in subduing him. Sometimes the boy went to Orléansville or Ténès to deliver a load of wood or charcoal, and there he envied the soldiers their life. These men knew what they wanted. He admired them for that, and for the fact that they were afraid of nothing—not even Allah—and could indulge in the worst debauchery, commit the bloodiest excesses, and always with laughter. To him the blue jacket meant freedom.

One day when his father had struck him, Kaddour ran off to Ténès and enlisted. Too late he discovered he had been wrong, and revolted. The solitary confinement and the beatings soon calmed him down. Later he learned that the soldier, who is a slave in the barracks, can be master outside, can bring terror to the hearts of private citizens, can get drunk, gamble, and go after women. Then he accustomed himself to that sort of life. He was not a bad soldier: on the quiet side at the barracks, but a complete good-for-nothing outside, and to be avoided when he had drunk.

And yet he had not been able to bring himself to reenlist. A vague desire had come upon him, a homesickness for his *douar*, for the great dark mountains with the sea behind them, where the horizon looked higher than the peaks. And now that he was about to be free, he was seized with anguish, and felt almost afraid.

Good-bye! Keep us in mind! Quietly the soldiers took leave of their departing comrade, and he went out, his head spinning. He felt drunk.

Immediately he left Ténès, where he had put in his last six months after returning from Laghouat. At the gateway of the town, he turned to glance once more at the big barracks that stood higher than the gray mass of ramparts, and looked out over the deep valley of the Oued Allala. And he recalled the many nights when he had stood here in the archway impatiently awaiting the arrival of some Spanish or Moorish servant-girl who had been attracted by his imposing physique and the finely modeled bronze mask of his face, or the fire that burned in his eyes. It was all over.

He went on. Above the gorges, scarcely moving their wings, hung the eagles, like golden nails affixed to the incandescent sky. He came to the true countryside. From the rounded backs of the dry hills he looked down across the bare plain to the dark spot where the village of Montenotte stood in its setting of eucalyptus trees.

It was the month of July. Not even a strip of green remained on the land's exasperated palette. The pines, the pistachio trees and the palmettos were like blackish rust against the red earth. The dried-up river beds with their banks that seemed to have been drawn with sanguine made long gaping wounds in the landscape, revealing the gray bones of rock inside, among the slowly dying oleanders. The harvested fields gave a lion-colored tint to the hillsides. Little by little the colorless sky was killing everything.

Kaddour had cut himself a stick of wild olive wood, which he held behind his head, gripping it at each end as he walked along, his chest thrust forward. It was good to be going along all by himself, free, weighted down by neither sack nor gun, and to be on his way home.

A military procession was passing somewhere in

the distance. First came the loud, indifferent bugles, and then the ear-splitting, drunken wail of the rhaitas. That too was over: he need no longer keep in step with the drums. Once again he felt a momentary anguish.

He came to the big carob trees of the square. Up on the rocky plateau stood the huts of blackish reeds, surrounded by gray thornbush. The Ouled bou Medina clan lived there.

Almost timidly the soldier approached his family's farm. Savage dogs rushed out at him; a young woman covered her face and fled. The large bony man with a profile like an eagle's was his father. When he saw Kaddour, joylessly he offered solemn praise to Allah. Mohammed and Ali, Kaddour's two small brothers, had grown into proud, tall youths. The beard was beginning to show on their faces, and a wild, reckless light played in their hazel eyes. They stood apart, indifferent to his arrival. Only old Kheira, his mother, burst into tears of happiness as she felt the shaved pate of her first-born.

She found an old gandoura for him, and a burnous and turban which had been his father's. Kaddour looked at his cast-off military garments and was ashamed of them.

In a dark corner sat Fathma, the wife of his brother Mohammed. She kept her face covered. Mohammed himself, wary of the stranger, wandered between the family's two huts. He did not dare hide his wife from his brother's sight, because such a thing was not done. But he felt a dull hatred for this man he no longer even recognized, who had engaged in the lowest of occupations, had partaken of foul infidel food and blasphemed Allah and the Prophet by drinking wine. This was the grudging welcome the soldier found at home.

The farmers of the region, as soon as they had finished what little work was absolutely necessary, spent their days sitting in the local café. When Kaddour walked in, they stared at him with vague distrust. Perhaps if he had just come out of prison they would have been better disposed toward him. A man is thrown into jail in spite of himself, whereas it is of his own free will that he becomes a soldier.

And so all the happiness he had felt on arriving home was dissipated. He understood that for these people he would always be the *askri*, the soldier, and that in their eyes he was virtually a traitor.

Life on the farm struck him as being uncomfortable. He slept on the ground and ate the hard black bread. The wood he had to cut grew in the midst of spiny scrub, and it was a long way to the town where he sold it. He built fires in the hills to make charcoal, and kept the thatch of the huts in repair.

He tried to go back to his old life of the nightly chase for amorous adventure. But only the wrecks, the ones who could be approached directly, were interested in the love of a soldier.

At home there was Mohammed's wife Fathma, lovely and languorous, with eyes that spoke of submission and tenderness. Kaddour had now regained the religious scruples of his people, so that at first the idea of having anything to do with her seemed such a monstrous crime that no Moslem could entertain it. But the hostility of the environment, Mohammed's growing hatred, and the violence of his own desire combined to break down his resistance.

Now that he was married, Mohammed constantly sought other women on the neighboring farms, often leaving Fathma by herself. She had noted her brother-in-law's interest. To her the soldier was a kind of hero because he had committed so many sins.

A hyena had been following the flock. One night when Mohammed was busy trying to track it down, Kaddour, armed with his knife, slipped into his brother's hut. Immediately, with no resistance whatever, she accepted him.

After that, nearly every night, with incredible brazenness, as soon as he knew that Mohammed had gone out, he returned to her.

The winter went by. Kaddour was still a stranger to his family. He had turned into an inefficient worker, and spent hours sprawled in the bush smoking, while the oxen dozed in the partly-plowed field. Ali also had married, and like Mohammed he mistrusted the soldier, not even bothering to hide the enmity he felt. The father, silent and unbending, showed his disapproval by never addressing a word to Kaddour. And in the village they looked down on him, claiming that sometimes he uttered blasphemous words. He felt himself to be in the way, detested, branded for all time, as if his flesh had been indelibly marked by the blue jacket.

The hot sun of spring burned the hillsides. For the past forty days not a drop of rain had fallen. In the faded fields wide reddish stains were forming, like terrible burns, or the ravages of leprosy. From all the villages scattered across the countryside rose great cries of despair. The sky arched above, perfect in its clarity, like a vast ironic smile. Another drought, like the one that had been decimating the farmers for the past two years.

In the Chenoui household poverty made the situation still more untenable. Kheira, the old mother, had died. The soldier was one too many.

One day the hatred that had been latent between them for so long suddenly sent Mohammed and Kaddour at each other, brandishing their knives. The old man separated them with a club. They stood there, trembling with rage.

And, notwithstanding the tears shed in secret by Fathma, Kaddour went out one morning without a word of farewell to his kinfolk, his heart hardened and closed in upon itself permanently. He walked along the road. The dry wind, completing its work of cracking open the earth, whipped against the muscles of his legs under the rags of his gandoura and his burnous. Gaunt, his eyes blazing, he was on his way down there, to the city, to wear the blue jacket and the scarlet fez once again.

Along the flanks of the burnt-out hills, across the dying crops, came a troop of children. The boys already wore turbans and were proud of their burnouses. The little girls had tattoo marks on their foreheads, and their eyes were like those of wild animals. They all went along, carrying a huge doll made of a stick covered with a red gandoura and a black scarf. Their slow sad song

os—c

was a prayer for rain.

The small figures went past, in all the glory of the devouring sun, performing their ancient ritual that was still intact after so many centuries. They passed by, and the condemned man continued along the dusty road, shrugging his shoulders.

Let the whole place go up in smoke! he thought. Down below in the barracks at least there's food.

Achoura

In the showcases that stand in front of photographers' shops, exposed to the stares of curious outsiders, you will find a picture showing a woman of the south. She is wearing bizarre garments, and her impressive face, which reminds one of an ancient oriental idol, perhaps, has something spectral about it. A predatory bird with eyes full of mystery. What singular daydreams, one wonders, and in the case of a few rare souls, what glimpses of foreknowledge of the stark, shining south have been evoked by this photograph of an "Ouled Nail" girl in the minds of the passers-by who have stared at it and been troubled by it?

One can scarcely imagine that the hidden life of this woman from another place, somewhere so near and yet so distant, might conceal a drama. Yet those shadowy eyes have seen the phantom called happiness, and the arched lips have smiled into the face of that phantom.

In the first place, the words *Ouled Nail* should not have been used in connection with the portrait of Achoura bent Said. Achoura, who possibly still exists in the back part of some Bedouin tent, was actually of the wild Chaouiya tribe that lives in the Aurès Mountains.

Her tale, eventful yet sad, is one of those Arab love

epics with an ancient setting, the product of a place where the unchanging society has no poets other than the shepherds and camel-drivers. With their intuitive ability to make art without artifice, these men improvise plaintive chants, as long and monotonous as the roads of the desert. Achoura's life could have been the subject of one of these songs.

Being a woodcutter's daughter, Achoura had passed the first part of her life merely living the unutterable dream of childhood, unconscious of the huge mountains and their dark cedar forests. Then, married off too young, she had been taken by her husband to Batna, a sad, dreary town full of barracks and abandoned houses, a town without a past or a history. Locked into the house, and bored with an existence she should never have had to undergo, Achoura suffered the pain that comes with longing for freedom. Her husband soon threw her out, and she went to live in one of the dilapidated huts of the Village Nègre, where she was at the service of the garrison.

There her strange nature became more pronounced. She was distant and haughty with the other women of the quarter as well as with her clients in their red jackets or trousers, whereas with the poor or the sick she was warm and outgoing. Like the others she got drunk on absinthe and spent endless hours sitting in her doorway, a cigarette in her mouth, and with her hands folded on her crossed knee. But she had kept that grave, melancholy air that was so much a part of her sombre beauty, and her eyes, fixed always on some distant point, revealed not thoughts but the flames of passion.

One day Si Mohammed el Arbi, the son of an important commander in the south, saw Achoura and fancied her. He was handsome, daring and capable of violent emotions, and he delighted Achoura. The only happiness available to her was bitter and painful, for he was jealous. It hurt his pride to think of her living as she did, there in the Village Nègre, in the lowest sort of promiscuity, at the mercy of the soldiers. But it would have caused a scandal if he had taken her out, and the young Cherif was afraid of his father.

As happens with love's creatures, Achoura felt a new life being born within her. It seemed to her that never before had she really seen the sun turn the crests of the mountains gold, and never before watched the capricious play of lights on the tufts of the trees. Because the joy was in her, she felt it coming up out of the earth.

Like all the women of her region, Achoura considered the sale of her body the only escape from want that was available to a woman. She had no desire to be cloistered again by marriage, nor was she ashamed to be what she was. To her prostitution seemed legitimate, and did not interfere with her love for her favorite. Indeed, it never occurred to her to associate in her mind the indescribable bliss they knew together with what she called, using the cynical *sabir* word, *coummerce*.

Achoura loved Si Mohammed el Arbi. It was her pleasure to provide him with primitive little luxuries. No one else ever lay on the white wool mattress she kept for the Cherif, and no other head but his was allowed to rest on the embroidered pillow. When she expected him, she went to the European florist and bought masses of sweet-smelling flowers which she spread over the mats, on the bed, and all around the humble room which bore no trace of the orgies to which it was regularly a witness. The miserable little hovel, ordinarily the scene of drunkenness, brutality and simple debauchery, became a delightful, mysterious retreat for lovers. And although with her clients Achoura was imperious, capricious and hard, when she was with the Cherif she became sweet and pliant, if not wholly passive. She was happy to wait on him, even to humiliate herself before him. She liked his naturally despotic manner; it was only his jealousy that was painful. The knowledge that she was common property offended his innate delicacy, but he was grudgingly willing to accept the fact, since he could not defy custom to the point of openly avowing a relationship that had become virtually marital. However, what he feared, and what drove him to terrible rages when he suspected it, was that she might *love* another man; it was the question of the sincerity of her relations with the anonymous men who shared her bed when he was not there. Like all the men of his race, he placed no trust in anyone, and thus was tormented by suspicion.

One day for no valid reason he became convinced that she was deceiving him. Because his suffering was real, his anger was terrible. He struck her and left her without a word.

Si Mohammed el Arbi lived in a solitary *bordj* in the hills, far from the town. Achoura went on foot through the icy winter night to ask his pardon. In the morning they found her outside the entrance to the *bordj*, lying in the snow. Si Mohammed el Arbi was touched, and he forgave her.

The young man's father came to hear of the liaison between his son and a woman of the district. He went to Batna, and without seeing Si Mohammed el Arbi obtained Achoura's immediate expulsion from the town.

She sought shelter in Biskra, in one of the tiny stalls of the rue des Ouled Nail, where, in spite of his father, Si Mohammed visited her at every opportunity. And since each of them had known suffering because of the other, the love between them grew sweeter and more human.

Lying on her mattress in the overpowering heat of the afternoon siesta, Achoura would lose herself in endless contemplation of a faded photograph of the adored face, which from time to time she would cover with kisses. All this helped to pass the hours until once more he would be by her side and together they could forget the pain of being separated.

But Achoura's happiness was short-lived. Si Mohammed el Arbi was given the post of *caid* in a prosperous region further south. When he left, he wrote Achoura that he would send for her so that she could live in Touggourt, where she would be nearer to him.

She waited patiently. The letters from the *caid* were her only consolation. Soon they began to arrive more rarely. Down there in that new place, in the midst of a new life, so different from the old life of idleness and dreaming, Si Mohammed el Arbi had fallen prey to other eyes and known other moments of delight. And the day came when he stopped writing altogether. For him life had just begun, whereas for Achoura it had just ended.

When at last she was certain that Si Mohammed el Arbi no longer loved her, a spark that had glowed within her was extinguished, and without it she was plunged into darkness. She became indifferent, morose, and took to drinking in order to forget. Then she returned to Batna, perhaps drawn there by fond memories. There in the purlieus of the quarter she met a spahi who fell in love with her, and whom she subjugated to her will without pleasure. Then, when the spahi had been demobilized, she sold most of her jewelry, keeping only the pieces that had been given her by the Cherif. She gave part of the money to poor pilgrims about to set out on the trip to Mecca, and the rest she spent marrying the spahi. He, being a gambler and a drunkard, was unable to live as a civilian, and was obliged to reenlist in the army.

Achoura withdrew into the shadowy anonymity of Moslem life, of which she had become a silent and exemplary member, at liberty now to dream of Si Mohammed el Arbi the handsome Cherif who long ago had forgotten her, and whom she still loved.

The Convert

A ruined stone farmhouse, a rocky field in the rough French Piedmont highlands, hopeless poverty in a family of twelve children. The early years of apprenticeship under a brutal master. A few images, vaguer, scarcely etched into his illiterate's memory, a few times when the sunlight had lightened up the blue peaks, a few quiet spots in the dark woods, on the banks of streams among curling ferns. That was about all that Roberto Fraugi could recall at the moment when he set sail for Algiers, with his comrades, who were all itinerant workers like him. Over there in Africa he would be working on his own, and could put aside a little money. Later he would go back to Santa Reparata, buy some good land, and there, raising what corn and rye he needed for himself, finish out his days.

But he felt lost, perhaps almost afraid, here on this burning soil with its dreary horizon. Everything was so different from what he had ever known.

He spent several years in the cities along the coast, where he found countrymen of his and where he could still be reassured by certain understandable facets of the social life around him.

The men in burnouses, who walked slowly and spoke an incomprehensible tongue, were to be avoided.

He distrusted them and so, although living in their midst, he remained ignorant of them. Then one day a native chief from the edge of the Sahara offered him a construction job in his bordj. The pay was good. There was no work to be found in Algiers. Roberto ended by agreeing to go, but only after long deliberation. The idea of travelling so far, of being in the desert and living for months on end with Arabs, frightened him.

Full of misgivings, he set out. After a trying trip in a carriage that creaked, he found himself at night in Msila. It was summer. The heat seemed to come up from the earth and enfold him. An indefinable odor hung in the air. He felt strangely uncomfortable standing there all alone in the square only faintly illumined by the great pale stars. Far off, in the country, the crickets were singing, and their immense sound filled the silence broken only now and then by the nearby croak of frogs from the ditches that lined the streets. In the distance there were the black silhouettes of young palm trees against the greenish-blue sky. Vague forms in white lay stretched out on the earth around him, men who had not been able to sleep inside their houses for the heat and the scorpions.

The following morning in the sparkling clarity of dawn, a tall sunburned Arab with sombre eyes came for Fraugi in his little hotel room.

I work for the caid. Shall we go?

The cool air of the open countryside was delicious. A vague, fresh scent rose from the earth. Behind them silence lay over the still sleeping town. Fraugi, perched on a mule, followed the bedouin, who rode a small shaggy grey horse that bounded joyously at each step. They crossed the river in its deep-cut bed. The new-born day gave color to the adobe houses and the unlikely shapes of the saints' tombs.

After the palm gardens of Guerfala, they came out onto the plain. It stretched before them, pink, empty, infinite. Far away to the south the Mountains of the Ouled Nail were barely visible, a diaphanous blue.

This plain is called the Hodna, said the native. And over there by those hills is Bou Saada.

Far out on the plain, at the bottom of a saline depression, they came upon a few ruined greyish walls and a crumbling mausoleum with a high, narrow dome. Farther up, on a stony swelling of the earth, stood the caïd's bordj, a sort of square fortress with cracked walls that once had been whitewashed. They passed a few stunted figtrees around a fountain. The warm pink water trickled into a canal lined with crooked piles of reddish salt and stacks of white saltpetre.

The mason was given a bare little bedroom, all white. In it there was nothing but a reed mat, a chest and a skin of water hanging from a nail. Here for six months or so Fraugi lived, far from all contact with Europeans, among the bronze Ouled Madbi with their eagle-faces and eagle-eyes, and around their heads the high *guennour* with its black cords.

Seddik, the young man who had gone to Msila to fetch him, was the foreman of the gang of laborers working under the mason. They were slow in their movements, and as they worked they intoned long, plaintive chants.

In the solitary bordj there was silence, broken only faintly from time to time by the gallop of a horse, the squeaking of the well, or the savage growl of the camels when they arrived to kneel in front of the main gate.

In the evening at the red hour when everything grew still, the men assembled on the heights above and prayed. Their gestures were all-embracing, their voices solemn. Afterward, when the caid had gone inside, the khammes and the servants squatted on the ground to chat or sing.

The people at the bordj were friendly and polite to Fraugi. Above all, they demanded practically nothing of him. Little by little, lulled by the pleasant monotony that life had assumed there, the desire to return to his homeland left him. He grew used to the slow rhythm of a life without care or haste, and since he now was beginning to understand Arabic, he found the natives simple and sociable, and as a result enjoyed living among them. He sat with them now on the hillside at the end of day, and questioned them about their lives, or told them about his country. Ever since his first communion he had neglected to practise his religion, because it left him indifferent. Seeing these men so calm in their belief, he asked to hear about their faith. What he heard sounded to him a great deal simpler and more humane than the religion he had been taught to believe, with its deliberately confusing mysteries.

Winter came, and the work at the bordj was finished. Fraugi began to think disconsolately of his approaching departure. The farm-workers and the laborers did not want to see him go. Here was a foreigner who was not proud, who did not look down on them. He was an *ouled-baba-Allah*, they said—a good man.

And one evening, as Seddik and Fraugi lay stretched out side by side in the courtyard near the fire, listening to a blind singer from the Ouled Nail, Seddik said to the mason: But why are you going? You have a little money and the caid likes you. Abdelkader ben Hamoud has left now for Mecca. You could rent his house. It has fig trees and a plot of good land. Besides, the men in the tribe have decided to build a new mosque and a mausoleum for Sidi Berrabir. That work would pay your living expenses, and everything would go on the same as before.

And in order that things might go on "the same as before," he agreed to stay.

In the spring, when they learned of Abdelkader ben Hamoud's death at Jiddah, Fraugi bought the small property, without even reflecting that this would mean the end of his dream of returning home. No longer afraid of the hot rude earth, he signed a pact with it for all time. He let himself fall so voluptuously into the languid tempo of events that he no longer bothered even to go into Msila. It was enough for him to stay where he was. His European clothing became ragged, and one day Seddik persuaded him to put on native dress. At first he felt as though he were in disguise. Then he found it practical, and grew used to it.

The days and the years passed uneventfully in the sleepy village. No trace of homesickness for his native Piedmont remained with him. Why should he want to go anywhere else when he was so well-off at Ain Menedia?

He spoke Arabic now, and even knew a few songs with which he accompanied the ever slower motions of his work.

One day, talking with Seddik, he unthinkingly called to witness the "god beside which there is no other," and Seddik exclaimed: *Ya Roubert!* Why don't you become a Moslem? We're friends now. If you did, we'd be brothers. I'd give you my sister, and we'd stay together.

Fraugi remained silent. He could not analyze his feelings, but he was convinced that in some way he was already a Moslem, since he found Islam more satisfying than the faith of his fathers. He went on thinking about it. A few days later, in front of Seddik and the elders of the village, he testified of his own free will that there was no god but Allah and that Mohammed was His envoy. The elders praised the Eternal. Seddik, in spite of his calm exterior, was deeply moved. He seized the mason and kissed him.

Roberto Fraugi was now Mohammed Kasdallah, and Seddik's sister, Fatima Zohra, became the convert's wife. Simply, with no display of religious zeal, Mohammed Kasdallah performed the duties of prayer and fast.

They waited in vain for him in Santa Reparata, but he never went back. Thirty years later, Mohammed Kasdallah, now a pious elder, regularly praised Allah and His all-powerful *mektoub*. For it had been written that the cottage and the field he had dreamed of owning were to be granted him, only they were not to be in Santa Reparata. He would find them under another sky and on different soil, in the Hodna country among Moslems, and surrounded by the vast sad horizon of the waste land.

Criminal

The center was newly created; they called it Robespierre. It lay at the bottom of a damp valley, bordered by red cliffs and high naked mountains. The land which was to be colonized had been taken from the territory of the Ouled Bou Naga, and its rust-colored fields were stony and arid. But the directors and inspectors and other functionaries from Algiers, charged with the task of "populating" Algeria, and interested in proconsular appointments, had never bothered to come and see the place.

For a month the paper piled up, expensive and useless, with an eye to giving a semblance of legality to what was in fact nothing short of the ruin of a great tribe, and at best a risky enterprise for the future colonists. Did it matter? In the offices of Algiers nobody gave a thought either to the tribe or the settlers.

On the western flank of the mountains lived the Bou Achour, who from time immemorial had occupied the best land in all the region. United by strict consanguinity, they still lived on their lands without ever having resorted to the system of inheritance.

But expropriation had come, and the authorities had begun a lengthy and complicated inquiry into the *legal* rights of each farmer to the piece of earth he occupied. To help them in this task, they had rummaged through the yellowed and mutilated documents of the qadis of long ago, and had managed to establish the degree of relationship of one member of the tribe to the next. Then using these discoveries as a basis for procedure, they divided up the indemnities to be distributed. Here again the farce of bureaucracy ended badly for the miserable farmers.

The autumn sun, almost without heat, shed its pale golden light over the shabby administration buildings. Nearby, a row of hastily built houses crumbled in decay, and clumps of grass pushed up from their faded tile floors. The gray flock of men sitting opposite the offices was the Ouled Bou Naga. They squatted there on the ground, resigned and passive, wrapped in their uniformly earth-colored burnouses. Visible in their faces were the various ethnic strains that go to make up the highlander: Berber profiles with thin features and the rust-colored eyes of birds of prey, faces weighted with black blood, flat-mouthed and hairless, Arab faces, aquiline and severe. Their turbans are held in place by thongs, and their garments, loose and flowing, vary their form according to the position or gesture of the wearer, giving them the look of belonging to another age. Without the ugly "European" constructions across the street, it would have been a timeless scene.

Mohammed Achouri was a tall thin old man with the face of an ascetic, his hard features set in an expression of constant preoccupation. He stood a bit apart from the others, rolling the yellow seeds of his rosary between his bony fingers. He was looking off into the distance, where a cloud of dull golden dust hung above the land.

In spite of their air of resignation, the farmers were worried, and scarcely spoke among themselves. The French were going to pay them for their land; they were going to keep the promise they had made before exerting the final pressure, the promise that had caused the farmers' poor simple eyes to shine with excitement. But the long wait had begun to tell on them. They had been called for Tuesday, and here it was already Friday morning, and still nobody had given them anything.

Every morning they came and waited patiently. Then they broke up into groups to go to cafés, where each one ate a piece of hard black bread brought from home, and spent a sou for a cup of coffee. At one o'clock in the afternoon they reassembled to sit along the wall and wait. At dusk they went away discouraged, murmuring words of resignation, and the red glow of the setting sun caught their torn garments and enhanced their slow suffering. Eventually many of them had neither bread nor money to stay on in the town. Some of them slept at the foot of the walls, rolled in their rags.

In front of the offices a group of men conversed and laughed. *Mokhaznia* and foresters gathered their great blue burnouses around them and discussed their experiences with women and alcohol. Sometimes a farmer came up to them timidly and spoke. Then, with the familiar evasive gesture of the hand, the *mokhazni* or the forester, who knew no more than they did, would answer: Wait!

The farmer would bend his head and go back to his place, murmuring: The only power is with Allah the highest!

Mohammed Achouri had been thinking, and now he was in doubt; he regretted having given up his land. It pained his peasant's heart to know that now he had no land.

Money?

First, how much would they give him? Then, what would he do with it? Where would he go to find another field, now that he had sold the plot of earth that had kept him alive?

At last, the caid of the Ouled bou Naga, a tall, sunburned young man, began to call out the names of the members of the tribe. He stood in the doorway of the office building with a paper in his hand. The farmers had risen, their burnouses making water-like movements. They wanted to greet their caid. Some of them kissed his turban, others his shoulder. But he shook them off with a gesture and began the roll-call. As they answered, with the traditional "na-am," or by saying: "Here I am," or even with the military "*Brèsent!*" they found themselves shunted to the right. Then the caid led them to the offices usually referred to by the generic term *Domaine*. He went inside and was given a chair. A *mokhazni* standing in the doorway called the Ouled bou Naga and let them into the room one by one.

Mohammed Achouri was one of the last to enter. A European clerk in a threadbare suit sat at a black desk which had been gouged with jackknife incisions. The *khodja*, young and myopic, adjusted his glasses as he stood translating.

"Achouri Mohammed ben Hamza. You are a third cousin once removed of one Ahmed Djilali ben Djilali, one-time owner of the land known as Oued Nouar, in the Bou Achour sector. You thereby have certain legal property rights over the *domaines* called Zebboudja and Nafra. All told, minus costs, you are thereby entitled as payment of sale to the sum of eleven and a half centimes. Since there is no such coin as the centime, here you are."

And the clerk placed ten centimes in the farmer's outstretched hand. Mohammed Achouri stood there, waiting.

Well, go on. Get out of the way.

But I sold all my fields, a wagon and a half of hay, and several acres of forestland. Give me my money.

You've got it. That's all there is. Next! Abdallah Taieb Djillouli.

But ten centimes is no money. By Allah!

Nom de Dieu d'imbécile! Get out of here! Fast!

The *mokhazni* pushed the farmer outside. Once he was in the street he bowed his head, knowing how useless argument always proved.

The Ouled bou Naga stayed on nevertheless, imagining that some ray of hope still remained in the dark weather of their lives. They had the bewildered and melancholy expression of sheep standing at the slaughterhouse.

Mohammed Achouri suggested they go and complain to the administrator. A small group of them talked to the office of the *commune mixte*, in the middle of the town. The administrator, a pleasant man, raised his hands in a gesture of powerlessness. "I can't do anything. I told them in Algiers it meant the ruin of the tribe. They wouldn't listen. They give the orders. We carry them out. There's nothing to do about it."

He felt ashamed as he was saying this, ashamed of the baseness of the work he was obliged to do.

Then, since the chief, who personally never had done them any harm, said that there was nothing to be done, they accepted their ruin in silence, and went off to the valley where from now on they were to be paupers.

What mystified them above all, because it seemed so unfair, was the fact that certain of them had received relatively large sums, even though they had been working pieces of land much smaller than others who had been given only a few coppers, like Mohammed Achouri.

A *mokhazni*, son of a farmer, explained the reason for the strange and unequal distribution of money.

"But what does it matter what relation you are to somebody who's been dead for a hundred years?" cried Achouri. "We all live together. They should give the most money for the most land."

"They give the orders. They know more than we do. It's Allah's Will."

Once he had spent the money he had got for selling his livestock, he had no way of keeping alive, and so he went to work as a hired hand for Monsieur Gaillard, who had acquired the greater part of the land belonging to the Bou Achour.

Monsieur Gaillard was not a bad sort—energetic, a

bit rough, and basically a good, honest man. He could not help noticing the openly sullen behavior of his new employee. The other members of the tribe who worked for him were also unfriendly, but not to the degree of this one. At the outset Mohammed Achouri had placed a great distance between himself and the Frenchman, to whose good-natured sallies he remained wholly impervious.

The day after they had gathered in the harvest, the farmers stood looking in anguish at all the treasure from their land piled there in neat stacks. And in the darkness of the clear hot night, the new barn with its riches went up in flames.

Suspicion pointed to Mohammed Achouri. He denied it, quietly, obstinately. They found him guilty. He was a simple, unyielding man who had been robbed and betrayed in the name of laws he did not understand. And he had directed all his hatred and rancor against the usurping colonist. Surely Monsieur Gaillard was the one who had tricked them, and who had decided on the insulting ten centimes they had given him for all that land. This Frenchman at least was within reach.

Mohammed Achouri believed that by setting the fire he had restored justice. Monsieur Gaillard was mystified. He racked his brains trying to imagine what he might have done to bring about such an attack. He had given the man work. . . .

They could not know that they were indivisible, both victims of the same grotesque and evil game. The lawmakers sat far away in their palaces high above Algiers. Crime, particularly among the poor and downtrodden, is often a last gesture of liberty.

Taalith

She remembered, as one recalls a particularly beautiful dream, a time passed on open slopes flooded with golden sunlight. She had been there, below the great mountains split by gorges that opened them here and there to the blue warmth of the horizon. There were whole forests of pine and cork-oak, dark and threatening, and dense thickets whose hot breath rose as mist in the transparent autumn air, or in the brutal drunkenness of spring. Green myrtle and oleander lined the banks of the peaceful streams that wound through the fig orchards and the grey olive groves. The translucent ferns were like smoke hanging above the bloody streaks of broken boulders by the waterfalls. The streams rushed by, murmuring in the summer sunlight, or roaring in the terrible winter nights. There she had played, breathing the healthy air, watching the sheep, her strong limbs almost naked in the sunlight.

Then with a shiver of pleasure she recalled the magnificent wedding, when she had been given to Rezki ou Said, the handsome young hunter she loved. And it seemed to her, as she looked back on them, that those bygone days had been utterly untroubled. Everything had taken on the qualities of her own intense happiness.

Suddenly, in one terrible moment, everything had

been destroyed, swept away, like a column of dust dispersed by the wind. One night some horse-thieves had killed Rezki with a bullet. Then had come the ghastly period of mourning when she had torn at her flesh, ripped her clothing, pulled out her hair and gouged her cheeks with her fingernails. Like the savage mountain women when they are hit by gunfire, she had howled. Next had come the death of her father, partly as a result of poverty and partly from his fear that the frail hut would be buried under an avalanche of snow, for it was a bitter winter. A few months after that Zouina, her mother, married a merchant who took both of them to Algiers.

And now Taalith was a prisoner there, in a pale-blue courtyard surrounded by colonnades. On the other side of the high walls were the alleys of old Algiers, dark and dangerous, with their Turks and Moors. She felt smothered there, in that unhealthy gloom among women who spoke a strange language, and who referred to her contemptuously as "the Kabyle." A fresh torture had begun then: her stepfather decided that she must remarry, and his choice of husband for her was his business partner, an ugly old man.

Taalith, still in love, felt her flesh crawl at the idea of being with the old man, and expressed violent refusal. When her mother spoke with her, telling her how young and attractive she was, in the hope of bringing her around, she said: "But I love Rezki!"

It was true. She loved the dead lover-husband; her flesh still had painfully sweet memories of him. But her mother's nerveracking insistence, combined with the brutal beatings her stepfather administered, eventually made her see the uselessness of further struggle. In any case, she loved the dead man and was faithful to him. She felt alone and incapable of loving again.

The dark face with its tattooed forehead, its delicate lips and its long sad eyes, took on a new aspect, grew unhealthily thin and set in its expression, and in her gaze there burned a strange fire. One day she said to her stepfather: "It is written. I shall do what you want me to do." Then, more silent and pale than ever, she waited.

◻ ◻ ◻

It was the night before the wedding. Little by little darkness had stilled the household murmurs. Taalith and Zouina were alone.

Taalith said, smiling strangely: Mother, I wish you'd dress me exactly as I'm going to be tomorrow. I'd like to see how I look, with my eyes ruined from crying so much.

Zouina, delighted by this resurgence of childish enthusiasm, began to hand the girl muslin undergarments decorated with gold lamé, gandouras of tinted silk. They she brought out her Kabyle jewelry, and set the bridal crown of silver and coral above the hennaed tresses. Around the lovely bare neck, above the heavy incised neckband, she twisted the necklaces of glass, coral and gold coins. She enclosed the supple waist in a wide silver girdle, hung bracelets on the wrists, and attached jangling *khalkhal* to the delicate ankles. A perfumed paste had been spread over Taalith's body; it had dried and hardened, and now she was encased in its warm scented shell.

Zouina, crouched on the floor, looked up at her daughter. "How lovely you are, gazelle!" she exclaimed, again and again. Taalith had taken up her looking-glass, and was examining herself. She went on staring at her reflection, as if in a trance, for so long that Zouina fell asleep. Then, removing the noisy anklets, Taalith went out of the room.

The moon's slanting rays touched the tiling. The courtyard glowed white with its light. Behind the pillars and arches the darkness was blue. It must be late, Taalith murmured. She felt feverish. Tremulously she pressed her burning forehead against the cold marble surface of a pillar. An unbearable pain had seized her throat, and silent sobs shook her from within, but no tears came.

The coral ornaments on her crown made a faint clicking sound against the stone pillar. She shivered, and stood up straight.

In a corner was the ancient Moorish well. She leaned for a moment over the black mystery of the hole. Then she climbed up onto the worn rim. For an instant she stood there erect, like a statue silvered by the moon. She shut her eyes, murmured a pious word or two, and let herself drop into the shadows below. A swish of silk, a click of jewelry, a muffled thud, a far-off splash, and the monstrous black water licked the slippery stones at the sides. Then everything was quiet.

Taalith had disappeared, wearing her bridal costume. It was said by everyone that she had run away to become a prostitute in some purlieu of the Casbah. But Zouina, her face haggard and lined with worry, guessed the truth, and begged to be lowered into the well on a rope. She went on about this to such an extent that it was thought wiser to seal up the well. Then Zouina clawed at the stone until she broke her nails and tore open the flesh of her hands. For days on end she stayed out there, calling Taalith's name, over and over.

A search was undertaken in the town, but it produced nothing. Then they reopened the well. A man went down, and found Taalith floating there.

They laid the body on the white paving-stones, and the pale sunlight of afternoon illumined the jewels that still clung to the swollen green flesh, to the loathsome mass of carrion that had been Taalith.

The Rival

One morning the melancholy rain ceased to fall. The sun rose up into a sky that had been washed clean of the murky vapors of winter, and was now a deep blue.

In the hidden garden the big Judas tree stretched forth its arms, laden with flowers of pink porcelain.

To the right were the hills at Mustapha, their voluptuous curves receding into the distance, to lose themselves finally in infinite transparency.

The fronts of the villas glistened with tiny gold sequins.

Far-off, the pale wings of the feluccas dotted the pattern of changing reflections that lay across the quiet gulf. The warm air passed by like a caress. There was a shuddering in the essence of things. It was then that the vagrant conceived the idea of waiting, of staying in one place, of being happy.

He shut himself away with the one he loved, away in the milky little house where the hours flowed by without touching, in a delicious languid stream, behind the carved wooden screens, behind the faded curtains.

Stretching before them was the grandiose stage-set of Algiers, inviting them to share in its tender death-throes.

Why leave, why look elsewhere for happiness? The vagrant had come upon the inexpressible, here in the shifting depths of his loved one's eyes, depths he plumbed for endless periods of time, until the unspeakable anguish of pleasure crushed them both beneath its weight. Why seek the great open air, when their narrow hiding-place looked out over the immense horizon, and when they could feel the entire universe within themselves?

All that which was not a part of his love now fell away from him and was swept into the nebulous distance.

He abandoned his proud dream of solitude, and with it the joy he had felt when he had found a chance lodging. He renounced the friendly road, that tyrannical mistress drunk with sunlight who had ensnared him, and whom he had worshipped.

For hours and days the hot-blooded vagrant let himself be lulled by the music of a happiness that tasted of eternity.

Life and the things of life seemed beautiful to him. Also he thought he had become a better man, for as a result of his relaxed will he had mistreated his brutally healthy body, and this had left him with a better temper.

In the old days of exile, under the crushing boredom of sedentary life in the city, it had been painful merely to recall the play of sunlight on open plains.

Now, lying on a bed warmed by the sun that entered through the open window, he could turn to his loved one and whisper into her ear, telling her about the country of his dreams, and his words had the sweet melancholy that is weighted with the scent of dead things.

The vagrant longed for nothing. He hoped only for the limitless duration of that which existed.

◻ ◻ ◻ ◻

The warm night fell across the gardens. A silence reigned, an immense sighing, the sigh of the sleeping sea under the stars, as it lay beside the hot amorous earth.

On the soft manes of the hills the fires blazed like jewels. There were flames that trailed off in golden chains along the coastline, and flames that flared up suddenly like uncertain eyes in the velvet shadow of the big trees.

The vagrant and his love went out and walked along the road, where there was no one. They went hand in hand, smiling, in the night.

They did not speak, because they understood each other better in silence.

Slowly they climbed the slopes of the Sahel, as the late-arriving moon came up out of the eucalyptus forests of the Mitidja.

They sat down on a rock.

The nocturnal countryside was bathed in a bluish light, and silver feathers trembled on the damp branches.

For a long time the vagrant stared at the wide white road that led into the distance.

It was the road to the south.

The vagrant's soul suddenly awoke. A world of

memories stirred within him.

He shut his eyes to blot out the visions, and his hand closed tighter on hers.

But in spite of himself he opened his eyes.

The old desire for the other mistress, tyrannical and drunk with sun, had returned.

Once again, in all the fibers of his being, he belonged to her.

One last time, as he stood up, he gazed for a long moment at the road; he had promised himself to it.

They went back into the living shadows of their garden and lay down silently under a great camphor tree.

Above their heads the Judas tree stretched forth its arms, offering the pink flowers that looked lavender in the blue of the night.

The vagrant glanced at his love beside him.

Already she was no more than a vaporous vision, something without consistence that would soon be absorbed by the clear moonlight.

Her image was indistinct, very far away, scarcely visible. Then the vagrant, who still loved her, understood that at dawn he would be leaving, and his heart grew heavy.

He took one of the big flowers of the spicy camphor tree and pressed it to his lips to stifle a sob.

¤ ¤ ¤ ¤

The great red sun had sunk into an ocean of blood above the black line of the horizon.

Swiftly the daylight went out, and the stony desert

was drowned in a frosty transparency.

In one corner of the plain a few fires were lighted.

Nomads armed with guns sat around the bright flames, and the long white folds of their burnouses moved in the firelight.

A fettered horse whinnied.

A man crouching on the ground, his head thrown back, his eyes shut as if he were in a dream, sang an ancient song in which the word for *love* alternated with the word for *death*.

Then everything grew still, and became a part of the immense silence roundabout.

¤ ¤ ¤ ¤

The vagrant lay rolled in his burnous facing a half-dead fire.

Relaxed, resting his head on his arm, he abandoned himself to the infinite sweetness of falling asleep alone on the ground, a stranger among simple rough men, in a nameless desert spot to which he would never return.

The Magician

Si Abdesselem lived in a decaying little stone house splashed all over with whitewash. The curved trunk of an old fig tree spread itself over the roof, hiding it with its mass of wide leaves. Two of the rooms in this shelter were already destroyed. The foundation of the other two rooms was slightly higher, and it was here that Si Abdesselem, penniless and proud, led his solitary life and carried out his strange meditations.

One room contained several chests packed with books and manuscripts from Morocco and the Orient. In the other a Moroccan rug covered part of a straw mat, and there were some cushions, a small low table of scrubbed wood, and a brazier onto which he sprinkled benzoin. Apart from a few cups, plates and cooking utensils, plus the books that lay everywhere, there was nothing more in the house.

In the ruined courtyard, around the great fig tree that shaded the well and the broken paving stones, a few jasmine vines grew, the only sign of luxury in this singular dwelling.

Outside stretched the hills and verdant valleys leading down to the white town of Anneba. The bluish domes and white gravestones of the nearby cemetery stood out against the deep green foliage of the fig trees.

The sun had sunk behind the mountains, and the fires of the summer twilight had gone from the great space that lay over the languid countryside.

Si Abdesselem stepped out into the courtyard to wash for the twilight prayer. It was going to be a fine, calm night, he thought, and he would go and sit under the eucalyptus trees on the banks of the Oued Dheheb. He was a man of some thirty years, tall and lithe under his ample white garments and his black burnous. A white veil framed his bronzed face with its long grave eyes. The features were ravaged by lack of sleep, but he was no less handsome for this.

When he had prayed and said the *dikr* of our illustrious Cheikh Sidi Abdelkader Jilali of Baghdad, Si Abdesselem went outside. The full moon was rising down there over the calm sea, on a horizon only faintly obscured by greyish rags of vapor. He walked along. The fierce dogs outside the nomad dwellings near the cemetery growled, their voices muffled at first, then rising to yelps as they ran.

Then Si Abdesselem heard something that sounded like a cry of fear from a woman. Astonished, although without altering his pace, he continued to the road that led to Sidi Brahim, and then he saw a Jewish girl in rich garments. Trembling, she leaned against the trunk of a tree for support.

Why are you out here alone at night?

I wanted to find the taleb they call Sidi Abdesselem the Moroccan. But I can't, and I'm afraid of the dogs and the graves.

So it's me you're looking for, he mused. At this

hour, and all alone! Come on, then. The dogs know me and the dead never come near a man who walks on Allah's path.

The Jewish girl followed him, saying nothing. Abdesselem could hear her teeth chattering, and he asked himself how this charmingly dressed and timid young creature had managed to come there alone and in the dark.

They came to the house and went into the courtyard, and Si Abdesselem lighted a smoky old bedouin lamp. Then he stood still and looked at his unusual visitor. She was tall and svelte, and in her pale blue brocade gown, with her graceful Moorish coiffure, she had a strange and troubling beauty. He noted also that she was even younger than he had thought.

What do you want? he asked her.

They told me you could see the future. I'm unhappy, and so I came to see you.

And why didn't you come in the daytime like everybody else?

What difference does that make? Listen to me, and tell me what to expect.

The fires of Hell, the same as for your whole faithless race! he said, but softly, almost smiling. He was thinking that this delightful apparition could relieve the monotony and silent boredom of his life. Once they were in his room, he said: Sit down.

Then she spoke. I'm in love with a man who's cruel to me. He's left me. Tell me if he's coming back.

Is he a Jew?

No. He's a Moslem.

Give me his name and his mother's name, and let me work it out like the wise men of my country.

El Moustansar, son of Fatima.

For a long time Si Abdesselem made figures and letters on a wooden writing-board. Then with a smile he said: Jewess, this Moslem who let himself be misled by your charming ways finally had the strength and the good sense to escape from you. But he'll be back.

The girl gave an exclamation of joy. This means money for you, she said.

Si Abdesselem thought: All the stolen wealth of your race would not be payment for the priceless, bitter treasure I'm giving you.

Now, Sidi, I want to know more. I'm Rakhil, daughter of Ben Ami. She took the piece of cane which the taleb used as a pen, and pressed it against her breast while her lips murmured rapid indistinct phrases.

It would be better not to try to know any more about what lies in store for you.

But why? No! Answer me! Tell me!

Very well.

He began his mysterious calculations once more. Suddenly his face showed great astonishment. He looked attentively at the Jewish girl.

Si Abdesselem had the soul of a poet, and it delighted him, the strange chance that had put his existence in touch with that of this girl. For, as he saw it, her life was going to be lonely and tormented, and it was going to end in tragedy.

Listen, he told her. And blame only yourself for your curiosity. You've ruined the man you love. He may not know it, but most likely it was his own instinct that made him leave you. But he'll come back, and then he'll know. Ah, Rakhil! Isn't that enough? Do I have to tell you everything?

The girl was shaking and her face was livid, but she gave an affirmative nod.

You'll pass an hour of delight and high hopes with him. Then you will die in your own blood.

The words were swallowed by the silence of the night, echoless. The Jewish girl had buried her face in the cushions. Finally she looked up and said: So it's true. A little while ago, when the sun was going down, I went to the old gypsy who sits at Bab el Khemiss and asked her. When she told me I didn't believe her. But now you tell me the same thing, only worse. Why should I die? I'm young. I want to live.

Yes, he thought. The butterfly with bright wings that lights first on one flower and then another, and doesn't know its end is near. But you wanted to know, and now you're like a heron standing in a swamp.

The girl rolled on the rug, sobbing. Si Abdesselem's natural curiosity and passion for examining things had been sharpened by solitude. He looked at her without pity. There was no reason to feel sorry for this Rakhil. Was not everything that was to befall her already written, and thus inescapable? And was it not a sign of her vulgarity and ignorance that she should bewail the fact that her life was to be out of the ordinary? After all, she would know more intensity and passion, and more would happen in less time, and she would be spared boredom and disgust.

Rakhil! he said. Rakhil! Listen to me. I am he who wounds and heals, he who brings awake and puts to sleep. Listen, Rakhil.

She lifted her head, tears coursing down her pale cheeks.

Stop crying and pay attention. It's prayer time.

From a niche high up in the wall Si Abdesselem took a book bound in gold-embroidered silk, kissed it piously, and carried it into the other room. Then in the courtyard he performed his evening prayers.

Rakhil, left alone in the room, sat hunched over, thinking dark thoughts, and bitterly regretting her decision to probe the future.

Si Abdesselem came back in, smiling. Didn't you know that you were going to die sooner or later?

But I wanted to be happy again, and die in peace.

He shrugged disdainfully, and she rose to her feet. How much do I owe you? she said. Her voice had grown hard.

He looked at her, saying nothing. Then, after a moment, he said: You'll pay me what I ask?

Yes, if it's not too much.

Then I'll take what I want. He seized her wrists.

Let me go! she cried, her face insolent. I'm not for you. Let go of me!

A ripe pomegranate on the ground. Whoever picks you up can have you. What a man finds is a gift from Allah.

No. Let me go! And she struggled with him, trying to scratch him, to slip out of his grasp. Inexorably he bent her toward the rug.

Rakhil's beauty helped the melancholy taleb pass one short summer night. And in the morning, when she was feeling the pain of being hopelessly in love with him, and he, dreamy and indifferent, told her she might go, she let herself fall in a heap before him, and began to kiss his feet.

Let me come back to see you! With you I can forget El Moustansar, and that way perhaps I can escape what you say is going to happen.

Si Abdesselem shook his head. No. You're not to come back again. Another time it wouldn't be the same. No, don't come back. Go on and live out your life, and I'll live mine.

☆   ☆☆   ☆

At daybreak, after the early prayer, Si Abdesselem often strolled under the eucalyptus trees along the banks of the Oued Dheheb, thinking of nothing, intent on the smiling landscape around him. Now, as the burning sun climbed into the sky, he glanced down at the ground. Stretched out on the shore of black pebbles lay a woman covered with pink brocade, with a voluminous shawl around her head and shoulders. He went nearer, leaned over and pulled aside the shawl. It was the Jewish girl, young and lovely, her lips drawn back in a grin of agony. A bayonette had been thrust twice into her breast.

Si Abdesselem stood up. He remained a moment, staring at the body as he recalled the details in the night of love he had obliged Rakhil to spend with him. Then, with the same measured step, he continued his stroll through the increasing brilliance of the morning light.

Pencilled Notes

A subject to which few intellectuals ever give a thought is the right to be a vagrant, the freedom to wander. Yet vagrancy is deliverance, and life on the open road is the essence of freedom. To have the courage to smash the chains with which modern life has weighted us (under the pretext that it was offering us more liberty), then to take up the symbolic stick and bundle, and *get out*!

To the one who understands the value and the delectable flavor of solitary freedom (for no one is free who is not alone) leaving is the bravest and finest act of all.

An egotistical happiness, possibly. But for him who relishes the flavor, happiness.

To be alone, to be *poor in needs*, to be ignored, to be an outsider who is at home everywhere, and to walk, great and by oneself, toward the conquest of the world.

The healthy wayfarer sitting beside the road scanning the horizon open before him, is he not the absolute master of the earth, the waters, and even the sky? What housedweller can vie with him in power and wealth? His estate has no limits, his empire no law. No work bends him toward the ground, for the bounty and beauty of the earth are already his.

In our modern society the nomad is a pariah "without known domicile or residence." By adding these few words to the name of anyone whose appearance they consider irregular, those who make and enforce the laws can decide a man's fate.

To have a home, a family, a property or a public function, to have a definite means of livelihood and to be a useful cog in the social machine, all these things seem necessary, even indispensable, to the vast majority of men, including intellectuals, and including even those who think of themselves as wholly liberated. And yet such things are only a different form of the slavery that comes of contact with others, especially regulated and continued contact.

I have always listened with admiration, if not envy, to the declarations of citizens who tell how they have lived for twenty or thirty years in the same section of town, or even the same house, and who have never been out of their native city.

Not to feel the torturing need to know and see for oneself what is there, beyond the mysterious blue wall of the horizon, not to find the arrangements of life monotonous and depressing, to look at the white road leading off into the unknown distance without feeling the imperious necessity of giving in to it and following it obediently across mountains and valleys! The cowardly belief that a man must stay in one place is too reminiscent of the unquestioning resignation of animals, beasts of burden stupefied by servitude and yet always willing to accept the slipping on of the harness.

There are limits to every domain, and laws to

govern every organized power. But the vagrant owns the whole vast earth that ends only at the nonexistent horizon, and his empire is an intangible one, for his domination and enjoyment of it are things of the spirit.

The Oblivion Seekers

—*Kenadsa*

In this ksar, where the people have no place to meet but the public square or the earthen benches along the foot of the ramparts on the road to Bechar, here where there is not even a café, I have discovered a kif den.

It is in a partially ruined house behind the Mellah, a long hall lighted by a single eye in the ceiling of twisted and smoke-blackened beams. The walls are black, ribbed with lighter-colored cracks that look like open wounds. The floor has been made by pounding the earth, but it is soft and dusty. Seldom swept, it is covered with pomegranate rinds and assorted refuse.

The place serves as a shelter for Moroccan vagabonds, for nomads, and for every sort of person of dubious intent and questionable appearance. The house seems to belong to no one; as at a disreputable hotel, you spend a few badly-advised nights there and go on. It is a natural setting for picturesque and theatrical events, like the antechamber of the room where the crime was committed.

In one corner lies a clean reed mat, with some cushions from Fez in embroidered leather. On the mat, a large decorated chest which serves as a table. A rose-bush with little pale pink blooms, surrounded by a bouquet of garden herbs, all standing in water inside one of those wide earthen jars from the Tell. Further on, a copper kettle on a tripod, two or three teapots, a large basket of dried Indian hemp. The little group of kif-smokers requires no other decoration, no other mise-en-scène. They are people who like their pleasure.

On a rude perch of palm branches, a captive falcon, tied by one leg.

The strangers, the wanderers who haunt this retreat sometimes mix with the kif-smokers, notwithstanding the fact that the latter are a very closed little community into which entry is made difficult. But the smokers themselves are travellers who carry their dreams with them across the countries of Islam, worshippers of the hallucinating smoke. The men who happen to meet here at Kenadsa are among the most highly educated in the land.

Hadj Idriss, a tall thin Filali, deeply sunburned, with a sweet face that lights up from within, is one of these rootless ones without family or specific trade, so common in the Moslem world. For twenty-five years he has been wandering from city to city, working or begging, depending on the situation. He plays the guinbri, with its carved wooden neck and its two thick strings fastened to the shell of a tortoise. Hadj Idriss has a deep clear voice, ideal for singing the old Andaluz ballads, so full of tender melancholy.

Si Mohammed Behaouri, a Moroccan from Meknès, pale-complexioned and with caressing eyes, is a young poet wandering across Morocco and southern Algeria in search of native legends and literature. To keep alive, he composes and recites verse on the delights and horrors of love.

Another is from the Djebel Zerhoun, a doctor and witch-doctor, small, dry, muscular, his skin tanned by the Sudanese sun under which he has journeyed for many years following caravans to and fro, from the coast of Senegal to Timbuctoo. All day long he keeps busy, slowly pouring out medicine and thumbing through old Moghrebi books of magic.

Chance brought them here to Kenadsa. Soon they will set out again, in different directions and on different trails, moving unconcernedly toward the fulfillment of their separate destinies. But it was community of taste that gathered them together in this smoky refuge, where they pass the slow hours of a life without cares.

At the end of the afternoon a slanting pink ray of light falls from the eye in the ceiling into the darkness of the room. The kif-smokers move in and form groups. Each wears a sprig of sweet basil in his turban. Squatting along the wall on the mat, they smoke their little pipes of baked red earth, filled with Indian hemp and powdered Moroccan tobacco.

Hadj Idriss stuffs the bowls and distributes them, after having carefully wiped the mouthpiece on his cheek as a gesture of politeness. When his own pipe is empty, he picks out the little red ball of ash and puts it into his mouth—he does not feel it burning him—then, once his pipe is refilled, he uses the still red-hot cinder to relight the little fire. For hours at a time he does not once let it go out. He has a keen and penetrating intelligence, softened by being constantly in a state of semi-exaltation; his dreams are nourished on the narcotic smoke.

The seekers of oblivion sing and clap their hands lazily; their dream-voices ring out late into the night, in the dim light of the mica-paned lantern. Then little by little the voices fall, grow muffled, the words are slower. Finally the smokers are quiet, and merely stare at the flowers in ecstasy. They are epicureans, voluptuaries; perhaps they are sages. Even in the darkest purlieu of Morocco's underworld such men can reach the magic horizon where they are free to build their dream-palaces of delight.

The Breath of Night

It is the time of evening when the rays of the setting sun pass through an air already cooled by the first breath of night, while the mud walls give off the heat they have stored all during the day. Indoors it is like being in an oven. You must be outside, and feel the touch of the first shadows. And for a long time I lie idly stretched out staring up into the depths of the sky, listening to the last sounds from the *zaouiya* and the *ksar*: doors creaking as they swing heavily shut, the neighing of horses, and the bleat of sheep on the roofs. And the little African donkeys bray, a sound as sad as protracted sobbing. And the sharp thin voices of the black women.

Nearby in the courtyard there is the sound of tambourines and guinbris, making an accompaniment to some very strange vocalizations. These seem less like music than like the cries uttered during love-making. Sometimes the voices die down and all is silent. Then the blood in the veins speaks, by itself.

Soon life starts up again. Mats, rugs and sacks appear on the roofs of the slave-quarters. The ear still listens for muffled noises, kitchen sounds, arguments going on in low voices, prayers being murmured. And the sense of smell is jarred by the odors in the smoke that rises from the confusion of black bodies below, where the flames flicker joyously in the braziers. There are other silhouettes in the doorways of the holy men. It is all here, the daily life of the *ksar*, like something I have always known, and yet always new.

Over toward the right, behind the Mellah, there is a patch of wall that remains lighted up until very late. Its reddish surface serves as backdrop for the curious plays of shadow that are projected upon it. At times they move back and forth slowly, and then they seem to go into a furious dance. After all other voices have grown silent and everyone roundabout has gone to sleep, the Aissaoua are still awake. As the night grows perceptibly cooler, the members of that enlightened brotherhood, the *khouan*, pound on the tambourine and draw strident sounds from the oboelike rhaita. They also sing, slowly, as if in a dream. And they dance beside the flaming pots of charcoal, their wet bodies moving to an ever-accelerating tempo. From the fires rise intoxicating fumes of benzoin and myrrh. Through ecstasy they hope to reach the final target of unconsciousness.

I hear something more. When even the Aissaoua have sunk into sleep, I still see moving forms. A breath steals across the terraces, disturbing the calm. I know. I imagine. I hear. There are sighs and catchings of breath out there in the cinnamon-scented night. The heat of rut under the quiet stars. The hot night's languor drives flesh to seek flesh, and desire is reborn. It is terrible to hear teeth grinding in mortal spasms, and lungs making sounds like death-rattles. Agony! I feel like sinking my teeth into the warm earth.

In the morning the west wind arrived suddenly. You could see it coming, raising high spirals of dust, black as smoke. As it moved toward us through the calm air, it made great sighing sounds. And then it was howling like a living thing. I had a fantasy of being lifted up and carried off in the enormous embrace of a winged monster, come to destroy us all. And the sand showered onto the terraces with the steady, small sound of rain.

Diary Notes — 1899

Biskra
July 14 (1899)

Since I was having dinner at the Hôtel de l'Oasis, Captain de Susbielle, whom I had met during the day, suggested that I join his convoy going to Touggourt. I accepted, but in the course of the evening as I was talking with the natives I changed my mind when I heard of the rude manner in which this officer treats the Moslems. I did not have time to check on their statements, but inasmuch as I want to learn what I can about the customs of the south, I could not take the risk of losing the sympathy of the natives. In the morning when Captain de Susbielle came to fetch me, I excused myself saying that I was obliged to remain in Biskra, having received letters from my family, who planned to join me here. He said he would wait for me at Chegga, the second stopover on the road to Touggourt.

July 18

Left (with Salah and Chlély ben Amar from Bou Saâda) for Touggourt. My companions are in no hurry to get started. We stay on until two in the morning at the Café Chéoui in the old quarter, sitting with the son of a marabout and some spahis, discussing the south.

July 19

Arrived at Bordj Saâda at 9 A.M. A leaden siesta in the heat after walking all night. Lazy on awakening. We lie around, doing nothing. Played cards with some Chaouiya (Berbers of the Aurès) whose caravan is camped near the bordj. It is understood that I am an educated young Tunisian traveling for his education and in order to visit the zaouiyas of the south.

At Biskra Lieutenant-Colonel Fridel at the Bureau Arabe inquired if I was not a Methodist. When he learned that I was a Moslem and Russian, he was nonplussed. Those who are not in the Sahara for their own pleasure can never understand why anyone would come, particularly "out of season." If people were as they imagine them to be, Fromentin would never have written *Un Eté dans le Sahara.* True, I am not Fromentin, but one has to start somewhere. And then I make the mistake of dressing like everyone else here.

The cheikh of the Chaouiya is a curious old man who is interested in studying. At 3 o'clock he asks me to give him a French lesson. We stop at the hour of the sunset prayer.

Arrive about half past eleven at Bir Djefair, where we sit in the courtyard of the bordj. The place is alive with scorpions. To begin my apprenticeship as caravan-follower, I filled the water-skin with some excellent well water, using my tin cup.

Left at half past two in the morning.

July 20

Got to Bir Sthil around eleven in the morning.

Good water. Quarrel with the guard. Fever, intense thirst. Found nothing to eat. (Have been living on bread since night before last.) Left again at 9 in the evening. At the telegraphic post south of Sthil met caravans of Chaâmba going from Barika to Ouargla. Cheikh Abdel-kader ben Ali, a model of graciousness, offers to take me along with him to Ouargla free of charge.

About one o'clock in the morning nearly lost my horse, and my life, in a sebkha (dried salt lake) to the west of the trail. At three got back onto land, and lent my horse to a Chéoui who was walking with us in order not be be alone. As if we were out strolling, we followed the plantations of the Société Française de l'Oued Rhir. Arrived at El Mraier at five o'clock. Left again at nine in the morning and took the wrong road. Rejoined the Chaâmba around midnight. Met two nomads, a man and a woman, being taken under guard by an armed black named Abdou Fay, to the djemmaa near Ourlana in order to be divorced. We all continued together.

July 22

About two in the morning we arrived at the spring called Ain Sefra. Rested a while with the divorcing couple. Started out again at five, passing through El Berd, and meeting up with the Chaâmba about seven. At nine we rested beside the first fountain of the oasis of Ourlana. I went up to the bordj, and found that Susbielle had left an order that I was not to be allowed to remain at the bordj more than 24 hours. A day of thirst and fever, passed in the shelter built for the troops.

Started out at sunset. Spent nearly an hour, looking, with the help of matches, for the only good spring at Ourlana, on the trail to Maggar. Found it, and watered my horse as well as some sick mules, with my pail. Changed the water in the skin. Back on the trail, had an altercation with the cheikh of Ourlana. About midnight met the commander of the Cercle de Touggourt, leaving for his vacation in a carriage. Some two hours later stopped to rest, feeling ill. All three of us were seized with vomiting attacks and dizziness. Slept in the middle of the desert on the sand.

A search for the animals when we woke up. The man from Bou Saâda tries to light a cigarette with a pistol shot. Lakhdar, who carries the bread and water, came along behind us with his mule.

July 23

Between two and four o'clock in the morning we cross the west end of the Chott Merouan. Arrived (Salah and I) at El Maggar at four. Had coffee at the Arab mess-hall by the post-office. Went to look for Chlély, and found him. Left El Maggar about six, and arrived at Touggourt around eleven. Slept all day. Spent the evening making notes on "Women of the South" with Smain the brigadier and some singers.

At four in the morning the Khalifa Abd el Aziz and Sliman came to fetch me to take me to see Captain de Susbielle. A two-hour meeting, violent at first, and later more courteous on his part. A polite but glacial refusal to allow me to proceed to Ouargla, that is, to give my guides permission to go with me. I spent until ten in the evening searching for the Chaâmba, in order to go with them, leaving my guides at Touggourt. Found Taib the Chéoui, who told me the Cheikh Abdelkader sent his greetings, and that he left for the south this afternoon around four.

July 25

In the morning went back to the Bureau Arabe and asked permission to hire guides in the Souf. Granted.

July 28

Went on horseback to Temassine.

July 29

Left at four in the afternoon for El Oued. High fever. Fell into the dunes near the market of Mthil. A black postal employee named Amrou has come along with us.

July 31

Two in the morning, set out with postal employee Bel Kheir. At mid-morning arrived at Ferdjenn, where found the brigadier Osman and the spahi Mohamed ben Tahar. A day of fever.

August 1

Left at half past two in the morning with Soufi guide Habib. At 9 arrived at Moiet-el-Caid. Had a nap. Left after sunset. Came to Bir Ourmès around seven in the morning, and spent the day in the cheikh's garden. Argument and fight between guides and the cheikh's sons. Passed the night out in front of the bordj.

August 3

Left at 5 A.M. Short rest at 4 in the afternoon in order to drink at Kasr-Kouinine. Unforgettable impression of the sun setting behind the great dunes.

In the morning at seven o'clock arrived at El Oued. A Moslem funeral procession was going on.

Letter to the Editor
of *La Petite Gironde*

When Monsieur Loubet, President of France, came to Algiers, Isabelle Eberhardt was among those invited to the press banquet. As was her custom, she wore the attire of a Moslem man, being entirely covered in white wool, with no silk embroidery, no other spot of color save the brown camel's-hair cords twisted tightly around her white Sahara-style turban. The presence of this young Moslem divinity student with the powerfully sculpted forehead and the long thin hands, the soft voice and slow speech, did not go unnoticed by the reporters who were following the presidential tour. Certain of them, poorly informed, sent back to their newspapers inexact information as to the identity of, and the life led by Isabelle Eberhardt, comparing her to the warlike Berber queen of the Aurès, La Kahéna, who rode from tribe to tribe preaching hatred of the conquerors. These reports were merely local calumny, disseminated by a few small-time journalists afflicted with arabophobia. Isabelle Eberhardt felt that she must set things straight.

—Victor Barrucand, in the Appendix to *Dans l'Ombre Chaude de l'Islam*. The letter was printed in the newspaper *La Petite Gironde* on April 23, 1903.

□ □ □ □ □

◻ ◻ ◻ ◻

The true story about me is perhaps less romantic, and surely more modest, than the legend in question, but I think it my duty to tell it.

My father was a Russian subject of the Moslem faith, and my mother was a Russian Catholic. I was thus born a Moslem, and I have never changed my religion. My father died shortly after my birth in Geneva, where we lived. My mother then stayed on with my great-uncle. It was he who brought me up, and he did so exactly as though I had been a boy. This explains the fact that for many years I have worn, and still wear, men's clothing.

I began by studying medicine, but I soon abandoned it, feeling myself irresistibly drawn to a writer's career. In my twentieth year (1897) I went with my mother to Bône in Algeria. Not long after our arrival she died, first having been converted to Islam. I returned to Geneva to care for my great-uncle. Soon he also died, leaving me a fairly large sum of money. I was alone then, and eager to lead the life of a wanderer, eager to explore the unknown. I went back to Africa, where I examined Tunisia and eastern Algeria, travelling alone on horseback. Subsequently I visited the Constantine Sahara. For greater convenience and also as a matter of esthetics, I grew used to wearing Arab clothing. I speak Arabic fairly well, having learned it at Bône.

In 1900 I happened to be in El Oued, in the far Southern Constantine. There I met M. Sliman Ehnni, who at that time was a *maréchal des logis* in the Spahis.

We were married according to the Moslem rite.

Generally in military territories, a dim view is taken of journalists because of their tendency to ask embarrassing questions. It was like that in my case: from the outset both the military and administrative authorities treated me with the utmost hostility. When my husband and I attempted to have a civil marriage performed in addition to the Moslem ceremony, permission was refused.

Our stay in El Oued continued up until January 1901, when, under the most mysterious circumstances, I was the victim of an abortive attempt at murder at the hands of a native maniac. In spite of my efforts to shed some light on this matter, when the case came to trial before the Conseil de Guerre of Constantine in June 1901, nothing whatever was accomplished in that direction.

At the end of the hearings, at which I had been obliged to appear as principal witness, I was suddenly expelled from Algeria. The expulsion order brutally separated me from my husband. Since he had been naturalized as French, our Moslem marriage was not considered valid. Fortunately the order did not exclude me from France as well.

I went to my brother's in Marseille, where presently my husband rejoined me. There, after some small research, we were given permission to marry. It was very simple. True, this was in France, far from the proconsuls of the Southern Constantine. We were married at the Mairie of Marseille on the 17th of October, 1901.

In February 1902 the term of my husband's reengagement in military service expired. He left the army and we went back to Algeria, where he was shortly offered the post of *khodja* (interpreter and secretary) at Ténès, in the north of the District of Algiers, an office he still holds.

That is the true story of my life. It is the life of an adventurous soul, one that has got himself free of a thousand small tyrannies, free of what is called *usage* a soul eager for the constantly changing aspects of a life far from civilization. I have never played any kind of political role. It is enough for me to be a journalist. I study life by being close to it, this "native life" about which so little is known, and which is so disfigured by the descriptions of those who, not knowing it, insist on describing it anyway. I have never engaged in any sort of propaganda among the people here, and it is totally ridiculous to state that I pretend to be an oracle.

Wherever I go, whenever possible, I make a point of trying to give my native friends exact and reasonable ideas, explaining to them that French domination is far preferable to having the Turks here again, or for that matter, any other foreigners. It is completely unjust to accuse me of anti-French activities.

As for the insinuations made by your *envoyé spécial* to the effect that I am antisemitic, I can only reply that besides being a contributor to *La Revue Blanche, La Grande France, Le Petit Journal Illustré* and *La Dépêche Algérienne*, of whose staff I am a member at present, I have also written for *Les Nouvelles* which, under the editorship of Monsieur Barrucand, has done so much in the fight to destroy antisemitism. I went to work on *El Akhbar* at the same time as Monsieur Barrucand when he took over that old newspaper to give it a line that was essentially *French* and *republican.* It is an organ that defends the principles of justice and truth, principles which must eventually be applied here to all, without distinction as to religion or race.

I hope, Monsieur le Redacteur-en-Chef, that you will see fit to print my rectification, and thus allow me the opportunity of defending myself. I consider my cause entirely legitimate.

Agréez, monsieur, à l'expression de mes sentiments les plus respectueux.

Isabelle Eberhardt

IN THE SHADOW OF ISLAM
Isabelle Eberhardt
978-0-7206-1911-5 • paperback • 200pp • £9.95

'Her perception of Islam as a future, and not a spent, force on the world stage has proved prophetic. In that, as in the rebel-without-a-cause about her, she has proved ahead of her time.'
– *Daily Telegraph*

'A compelling narrative and an ideal starting point from which to discover more about Isabelle Eberhardt's picaresque life.'
– *Times Literary Supplementl*

In the Shadow of Islam is an extraordinary evocation of the desert and its people by a woman who dressed as a man in order to travel alone and unimpeded throughout North Africa.

In 1897 Isabelle Eberhardt, aged twenty, left an already unconventional life in Geneva for the Moroccan frontier. Gripped by spiritual restlessness and the desire to break free from the confinements of her society she travelled into the desert and into the heart of Islam.

Her experiences inspired a profound self-examination, and *In the Shadow of Islam* is regarded as one of the true classics of travel writing.

Peter Owen books can be purchased from:
Central Books, 99 Wallis Road, London E9 5LN, UK
Tel: +44 (0) 845 458 9911 Fax: + 44 (0) 845 458 9912
email: orders@centralbooks.com

www.peterowen.com

PRISONER OF DUNES
Isabelle Eberhardt

978-0-7206-0944-8 • paperback • 200pp • £12.50

'A masterfully evocative writer.'
– *Publishers Weekly*

'Evocative glimpses into Eberhardt's
fiercely nomadic life.' – *Blitz*

'Eberhardt has emerged from the shadows
and become a cult figure and an icon of
the women's movement.'
– *Publishing News*

Prisoner of Dunes is a selection of writings from one of the
most extraordinary female authors in history. Isabelle
Eberhardt lived only to the age of twenty-seven, but in that
short time she lived the kind of picaresque life that led her to
be dubbed 'the first hippy' – and left behind a remarkable
body of work documenting her encounters with North Africa
and Islam at the turn of the twentieth century.

Prisoner of Dunes spans her North African sojourns and a
period of exile in Marseilles. The essays explore the tensions
in her life that drove her and vividly evoke some of her more
singular experiences in her quest for freedom. Perhaps the
most unusual travel writing from any woman in the
twentieth century, this is its first appearance
in English translation.

Peter Owen books can be purchased from:
Central Books, 99 Wallis Road, London E9 5LN, UK
Tel: +44 (0) 845 458 9911 Fax: + 44 (0) 845 458 9912
email: orders@centralbooks.com

www.peterowen.com